Betty-Anne's

HELPFUL HOUSEHOLD HINTS

Betty-Anne Hastings
with Mary-Beth Connors

INTRODUCTION

How do you remove the odor of garlic from your cutting board? What's a quick tip to make your tires last longer? After slicing onions, does the smell linger on your finger tips? Do you know how to remove coffee stains? Do you even know how to find out?

As I'm sure you'll all agree, everyday life is fraught with enough minor traumas, small tragedies, and major headaches that the addition of any element that will make it run smoother is more than welcome. Well, here it is.

I have compiled in my Helpful Household Hints Book some of my favorite tips. A lot are little discoveries I've made over the years, trying to make life run a little smoother. Some are from friends; some are from friends' friends. Still others are adaptations and improvements on hints I've read in magazines, or remembered from my mother and her mother. They are not, by nature, national. I'm sure they come from all over the world. I know that people everywhere are interested in spending less time and money making their everyday existence easier.

To make it easier to find things in the book, I've divided everything into sections. The kitchen hints comprise one section, while Beauty Aids are grouped in another and laundry tips in still another. There is a section for virtually every part of the household. I've even included a whole section on stains, because they are a particularly difficult problem. With the price of clothing today, no one can afford to have an otherwise fine garment ruined by an accident.

This book is designed to save you money, in several different ways. First, by cutting your costs. For instance, did you know that expensive blue window cleaners are mostly just ammonia? For the same price, you can have twice as much ammonia, and your windows will be just as clean. If you must have the cleaner blue, just add a couple of drops of blue food coloring.

Secondly, <u>Helpful Household Hints</u> saves you time. I have interspersed the book with all kinds of time saving hints and tips. For instance, you may not know it, but there is a quick way to clean your venetian blinds, **and** save your hands! Simply use some string to tie a sponge around one end of a ruler. Presto! You've got an instant blind cleaner that cuts down on the time you spend cleaning and keeps you from acquiring all those cuts and scrapes we all associate with washing the blinds.

Last, I've tried to give you convenience. I've assembled every hint and tip I could think of in one easy-to-read source. The tale of contents is divided into chapters, with a brief description of what's in each one. If you're looking for something special, you should be able to find it quickly and easily.

The tips I've assembled are essentially the ones I've found most helpful over the years. The friends, neighbors and relatives I've shared them with have all, I think, found them helpful, too. I'm sure that you'll find that they lighten the load of your day, too. At least, I'm sure you'll find that they make everything run just a little smoother.

- Betty-Anne

Betty-Anne's Helpful Household Hints

CONTENTS

hints on how to remove many common stains and save on your cleaning bills.

7. **Laundry Lighteners**

Clothes that are well cared-for and laundered properly, are clothes that last. Here are some great tips for taking care of your laundry.

8. **Taking Care of Your Home**

You may not want to re-roof your house, but here are an assortment of basic tips for home repair that anyone could accomplish.

9. **Car Care**

Basic maintenance of your car can add years of breakdown free use to car life.

BEAUTY AIDS
AND
PERSONAL APPEARANCE

"Beauty", so the cliche goes, "is only skin deep", but when that skin belongs to you, it changes the meaning, somewhat. Let's face it; all of us want to present the best possible appearance we can. That's not vanity necessarily, but it is certainly an awareness of the image we broadcast to others and the negative and positive ways this image is received. In America, in the 1980's, all of us are judged by how we look, and more importantly, we all **feel** better when we look our best. The price, however, of keeping ourselves gorgeous is becoming prohibitive.

Cosmetic counters are full of products that moisturize the skin, relieve dandruff, or deep-scrub your skin. Most of them do what they say they'll do, but they have price tags that may stop your heart before they alleviate your wrinkles.

In this chapter, we've attempted to gather a potpourri of "home-made" cleansers, shampoos, conditioners, moisturizers and other beauty products that you can make at home, with common items from your refrigerator and medicine cabinet. Why pay those high prices when you can make products at home that are every bit as good for a fraction of the price?

Here are some suggestions:

A hot-oil treatment for your hair. Depending on the length of your hair, use between a fourth and a half cup of olive oil to massage and permeate your hair. Take a vaporizer and place a towel over it until it is damp with steam and very hot. Wind your head in aluminum foil to seal in the oil and allow heat to build up under the foil. This will aid the saturation of the oil into the follicles. You can secure the foil to your head (if necessary) with hair-setting tape. Next, wrap the steamed towel around the foil and go on about your household business for one half-hour or so. When you wash out the oil you'll have healthier, happier hair.

The next time you reach for an expensive hair rinse, don't! Try rinsing your hair with a mild solution of lemon juice, vinegar, or flat beer. Just mix two or three tablespoons of any of the three with lukewarm water; about half a cup. Pour through your hair, let stand for a few minutes, and rinse out. You'll find that they all remove soap film and leave your hair shiny and bouncey.

Try these two foods for a great cream conditioner. Take one-fourth cup of real mayonnaise and half an avocado. Place both of them in the blender and cream them together. If you are a blond, add a tablespoon of lemon juice to bring out the highlights in your hair.

After shampooing, work the mixture through your hair and leave it on for five or ten minutes. You'll find that what you may have thought of as "salad dressing" brings a healthy shine to your hair.

Have you ever considered a fresh egg conditioner for your hair? The next time you have a recipe that calls for egg whites, don't wonder what you'll do with the yolks: they make a great conditioner. Just wet your hair and towel dry it slightly. Use a fork to whip the yellows and blend in a little milk. Work the mixture into your hair and let it stay for about five minutes. Rinse it off and shampoo. You'll be amazed at the results.

Tea can be a great pick-me-up for tired hair. Natural, fresh smelling cammomile tea, brewed and allowed to become tepid makes an excellent rinse. Pour it through your hair after shampooing and allow it to stay on for five minutes or so before rinsing it away. Your hair will be healthier and happier afterwards.

Have you ever considered how bad it is to set your hair every day with hot rollers? Of course, hot rollers give you a quick, deep set that you can't get the old-fashioned way, but they can make your hair brittle and dry after prolonged use. Here's a tip; try setting your hair dry, and covering it with a damp steamed towel for a few minutes. You'll get a quick, deep set and save your hair, too.

You probably have one of the world's

best eyecreams in your medicine chest already. Vaseline will do everything those fancy heavily-advertised eye creams will do, at only a fraction of the cost. All you will miss is the fancy packaging. <u>Petroleum jelly also makes a great full-face moisturizer.</u> Try rubbing it in with plenty of mineral water to dilute it and make it less greasy.

Are your eyes tired after a long, hard day? Well, relieve them with items you can find in your own refrigerator. The next time you have a cup of tea, save the bag and keep it chilled. You'll find that a cold tea bag will do wonders for your tired eyes. Tea bags will also take away the puffiness and help get rid of those dark circles that are ruining your looks. <u>If your eyes are red, here's a solution that doesn't involve expensive eye drops.</u> Simply cut slices of chilled cucumber and apply it to the lids. You will notice the redness and tired feeling fading from them within minutes.

Are you troubled by bad skin? Put some chilled apple cider vinegar into a spray bottle and "mist" your face, just as you would a plant, after you've scrubbed it clean each morning. Don't wipe it off, but allow the vinegar to dry naturally. It will tighten your face and leave you feeling refreshed.

Spray bottles will work with every kind of beauty aid, not just vinegar! You'll find them a cheap and indispensable aid to your beauty regimen.

Mineral water makes a great face freshener! Just load a spray bottle with chilled mineral water and "mist" your freshly washed face. It will "plump" your skin and invigorate you just as more expensive, bottled or canned waters will, at only a fraction of the cost.

Also, your spray bottle with mineral water, when applied lightly, will set your make up.

Lemons make a great soak for your hands. Just squeeze a half a lemon and a teaspoon full of glycerin into a cup of warm water. Soak your fingers for 3-4 minutes before drying and pushing back the cuticles.

Did you know you can make your own dry shampoo? Baby powder, corn starch, or cornmeal, all mixed with a little salt make excellent dry shampoos. Just put a half cup of any of the three into an ordinary flour sifter along with a healthy tablespoon of salt. Sift it into your hair and comb it through. Wait a few minutes and comb out the dirt, and you'll have a clean head of hair.

You can make your hair-setting lotion. Just load a spray bottle with a can of stale beer. You'll find it makes a great setting lotion, and will add sparkle to your hair. <u>Gelatin will also give you a great set</u>. Just dissolve a packet in a cup of warm water and use it in place of regular setting lotion.

Want a quick tip to handle a problem blemish? Are you bothered by occasional pimples that mar your complexion? Well, forget about all those high-priced, over-packaged blemish cremes. Try rubbing your blemish with a lemon rind or using a cotton-tipped swab to apply a little lemon juice and you'll soon be rid of your problem spot.

Here's how to keep the scent from your favorite perfume lasting longer. Simply mix a drop of your favorite scent with a dab of Vaseline and work it into your skin in the areas where you always dab your perfume. You'll find the scent lasts twice as long!

You can make your own deodorant at home. Simply fill a small spray bottle with luke-warm mineral water. Mix in a heaping tablespoon of alum and a generous dose of your favorite scent and shake well. Now you have a home-made version of what you pay so much for in drug stores.

Ever wish you could make your own facial scrubs? Simply make a light paste of cream of wheat, a little sugar and warm water. Allow it to begin to dry on your face and then very lightly rub it away with a damp cloth. The sugar will act as scrubbing granules, like sandpaper, so be careful how much you add or it will irritate the skin. Be especially careful of the tender, delicate skin beneath your eyes.

Quick hints:

To set your nail polish, plunge the dried nails into a large bowl of ice water for 30 or 40 seconds. The dip will keep your polish chip-free longer.

Baking soda, sifted onto your skin after a light spraying with mineral water will relieve a sunburn.

A light mixture of lemon juice or vinegar with mineral water is also good for sunburn pain.

Tired of throwing away your lipstick when you accidentally break it? Next time, try holding the halfs above a low flame. Once they are tacky, not melting, quickly join them and then plunge the lipstick into a bowl of ice-water for thirty seconds. Your lipstick will be good as new.

Store your lipsticks, nail polish, and foundation in the butter section of your refrigerator to keep them fresh and prevent them from drying out.

Baking soda, lemon juice, and fresh strawberries mixed in a blender to a paste make an excellent teeth whitener.

Lemon juice dabbed onto cold sores

will rid you of these troublesome spots in no time.

Lemon peel makes a great buffing agent for your nails.

The most important quick beauty tips of all: remember that all the hints and beauty aids in the world are no substitute for good posture, a healthy smile, and a happy attitude. Exercise, sunshine, and good food are not replaceable in your beauty regimen.

THE HOUSEHOLD

As we all know, traditional male and female roles and their relationships to our homes and home-lives are changing. It is not just women anymore who are besieged with making a household work on a limited budget. More and more men are being saddled with a responsibility they used to consider paultry. It is no longer easy to run a growing home on a limited budget, and from here, it doesn't look as if it will get any easier in the near future!

In this section, we've compiled an array of household hints to not only make your job easier and less time-consuming, but to lighten your budget worries too!

If you have them, you know that washing venetian blinds is a real chore. You've probably nicked, cut and scraped your hands a thousand times whenever you've had to wash your venetian blinds. Undoubtedly, it's your least favorite household cleaning chore. Well, here's a suggestion that may end all of that.

Next time you clean your blinds, try running your shower over them to wet them down and loosen the dirt. Next, get a foam "mitt" that's normally used to wash cars and squeeze some of your detergent onto it. You'll keep your hands safe and clean the blinds thoroughly at the same time. To rinse, simply turn on your shower again.

Ever wondered how to clean piano keys? Try soaking a piece of soft cotton flannel or chamois in a little de-natured alcohol. Rub the keys briskly with the damp cloth and then wipe them clean with another soft cloth.

Is the finish on your old wood furniture dull and lusterlous, regardless of how many times you wax it? Well, here's a wonderful tip to give your furniture a great shine without expensive refinishing. Make a solution of three quarters of warm water and one quarter of white vinegar. Take a clean, soft cotton cloth and gently rub the furniture down after you've soaked the cloth in the solution. If you do this fairly early in the day, and let the solution remain on the wood the entire day, you can wipe it down again with a dry cloth the following day. You'll find that when you polish it this time, your furniture will shine like new.

Want to speed up the process of polishing your wood furniture? Just heat the wax or polish container in a shallow pan of boiling water before you apply. You'll be surprised how quickly it goes on.

Tired of your windows streaking when you wash them? Try using wadded newspaper after you've washed them to take off the streaks and finish drying them. You'll find it a lot cheaper than paper towels and a lot less frustrating!

Here's a quick tip for repairing your ripped or torn window shades. Simply take down the shades and place them on a work surface. As you hold the sides of the tear together, apply several thin coats of clear nail polish to cement the ends.

This is a sure cure for your sticky windows. Just take a small (one inch) paint brush and "paint" the window tracks with a thin coating of Vaseline. The jelly won't freeze, and your sticky windows will be gone.

Troubled with small nicks on your furniture? Granular, instant coffee, mixed with a little water and applied with a clean, cotton cloth will cover those marks.

Kitty litter can absorb those ugly oily spots. Those spots of oil and dirt that spot your garage floor can be easily absorbed. Just sprinkle kitty litter over the spots, wait a few hours and sweep. You'll whisk away the mess!

But what about the stains, afterwards? Easy, just get a large bottle of mineral spirits at any hardware store and saturate the stained area. Cover it with old newspapers or more kitty litter and let it stand for two or three hours. After you sweep it away, you'll notice the stain has lifted. Scrub your floor with a light detergent solution afterwards.

Here's how to make your own furniture polish. Go to your local hardware, and get a bottle of boiled linseed oil and some turpentine. Mix equal parts (about one half cup) of each along with an equal amount of white vinegar. Place all the ingredients in a capped jar, seal tightly and shake well.

Are you upset about your drooping seat? I mean, the drooping seat on that beautiful cane chair you've had forever? Well, here's a little secret for tightening it up. Simply soak down the caning in a light solution of steaming, hot water and lemon oil; then place it in the sunlight to dry. The caning will shrink back to its original shape and the lemon oil will keep it from becoming brittle and cracking. After it's dry, apply another, more liberal coating of oil and let it sink in. Your chair will be good as new.

Have you ever been faced with dilemma of getting paper that's stuck to the surface of a table or chest off? Here is an easy solution. Instead of scrubbing or using solvents that ruin the finish of the surface, try putting a few drops of oil on the paper, and loosen it. A soft, cotton cloth will then remove it. Go ahead and oil the entire surface to make the finish even. It can be polished, if you like, after a few days.

If you have dark wood furniture here's a tip for dealing with those annoying little

scratches. Simply coat them with a little ordinary household iodine and watch them disappear.

If you wash your drapes at home, do you know how to press them? It's probably the best idea to always have your drapes and curtains dry-cleaned, but if that is too expensive or inconvenient and you wash them at home, here are a few tips on pressing them. Never iron rayon or synthetic draperies on the side that shows. You'll get that shiny look, like the seat of an old, worn-out suit. Instead, press them on the "wrong" side, using only a warm iron. You'll get out the wrinkles and save your expensive drapes. Any natural fiber can be ironed on the correct side with a hotter iron for the best results.

Do your drapes hang "wrong"? Are they lifeless, or do they hang in clumps? Try weighing the bottoms with old washers to give them a crisp, new line.

Add a little heft when polishing your furniture. Simply wrap your soft, cotton polishing cloth around a two or three inch scrap end of a two-by-four and see how much easier it is to achieve a sparkling shine, and save your strength.

You can clean your marble tables and surfaces, and even remove stains. Simply squeeze lemon juice onto the stain or the entire surface and work it into the marble with a thick, soft cloth. As soon as you see the stain "lift," rinse the top with mineral water.

Did you know that you can remove water spots from your fine wood furniture at home and without refinishing? Simply take an old, worn-in tooth brush and some baking soda. Wrap the bristles in a soft, damp cloth and dip in the baking soda. Rub gently to remove the water spot.

If your marble tables are un-stained, but you'd like to clean them, try this. Simply sprinkle the table-tops with baking soda and, using a spray bottle, soak the baking soda with mineral water. Allow it to remain on the marble for one or two minutes before removing it with generous amounts of warm water and an extra-soft cloth. When it drys, you can shine it with a marble wax or polish.

Here's a quick tip for cleaning up those soiled spots on your light-colored cotton upholstery. Purchase a gum or soft eraser at any art or hobby store. If it's the crumbly kind, simply "erase" the dirty area and suck-up the eraser shavings with your vacuum. If you've gotten the gummy, rubber kind, you will not have to vacuum, but you will have to be more careful. Do not work the eraser back and forth as you would an ordinary eraser, but work it in one direction only. You'll pick off the spot in no time.

Erasers can be used on your floors

too. They'll remove black heel marks and heel marks on your hardwood floors, too.

Remove cat or dog hairs in a jiffy. Simply dampen a thin sponge in a very, very light solution of warm water and glycerin. Wring out the sponge thoroughly and brush furniture lightly with it. It will pick up those pesty dog-hairs and cat-fur in no time.

Here's an alternative to polishing your silver. Fill a rubber dishpan with hot water, a liberal dose of table salt and a tablespoon of baking soda. Let your silver soak for fifteen minutes and then rinse in tepid water and dry.

Lemons can make your glass top tables sparkle. Make a solution of lemon juice and warm water to wash your glass-top tables. Dry them with a linen towel and then, as with your windows, go over them with a crumpled newspaper to remove all lint and make the glass sparkle.

Here's a suggestion to keep your tables from being scratched. Just buy ordinary felt and glue it onto the bottom of ashtrays, vases, and collectables. That way, their sharp edges will not mar your woodwork. Glue or double-faced tape will secure the felt.

This will keep your floors from getting scratched. Just as we've shown you how to keep your table-tops scratch free with felt, here's a solution to those annoying scratches chair legs and the rungs of rockers leave on your floor. Coat the bottoms of chairlegs and the length of the undersides of rocker-rungs with a double coating of one-inch masking tape. It won't show, and it'll keep your furniture from marring your floors. <u>Likewise, you can keep casters from scratching your floors</u>. Just coat the rolling part of the caster with masking tape and your worries about scratches are over.

If you just want to remove fingerprints from furniture, but you don't want to wax, here's how. Instead of using a wet cloth and clouding or dulling the finish on your furniture, soak a soft cotton cloth in vegetable oil and wring it out until it is virtually "dry". Wipe the furniture, moving the cloth in one direction only, not back and forth, over the surface of the piece to remove the prints. Wait a few moments to allow the oil to soak in, and then wipe off the oil with another soft cloth.

Want to keep you bed-linens and sheeting white? Don't bleach the bedclothes until they fall apart. Instead, try this trick; it's as old as the hills, but <u>everyone's</u> grandmother can't be wrong!

Light is what usually yellows bedclothes during their "lifetime". Early Americans painted the insides of their linen chests

28

and closets a dark blue to keep their sheets white, and it worked. Why not try it?

Has your best glassware ever burst when you poured hot liquid into them, or washed them in water that was too hot? We have a solution. Everyone learned in junior high school that silver will conduct and absorb heat quicker than glass. Simply place a spoon in the glass before pouring in the hot liquid, and insure yourself against loss.

Are you stymied as to how to clean vinyl furniture? This should relieve your confusion. Make a strong solution of vinegar and hot water and wash the furniture with a stiff heavy piece of woolen cloth. Once you've gotten off most of the grime, you should rinse the vinyl with warm water. Another easier washing with a very mild detergent may be desirable.

Wondering how to clean your washable walls without wearing yourself out? Here's a little trick a friend of mine learned in the navy. Just use an ordinary sponge with a squeeze attachment. You'll be able to really clean walls and even reach those awkward corners without knocking yourself out. You'll be surprised how quickly it will go, too.

Do your lightweight shower curtains fly around when you turn on the shower? Sew a magnet into the hem on each corner, and even put one in the middle if it bothers you. This will keep your shower curtain from flapping around.

If your slip-covers are washable, don't dry them completely. Place back on your furniture while they are still damp. They'll fit better and won't require ironing because as they finish drying they conform to the shape of the furniture and stretch out their own wrinkles.

Want to keep your piano in tune longer? Well, simply play it then. Although it may seem obvious, most people believe that pianos that are left alone stay in tune longer. In fact, a piano that is played retains its tuning far longer. So play, and avoid the expense of tuning your piano.

Did you know . . .

Lack of humidity and cold temperature are the two most prevalent causes of brittleness and cracking in your wicker furniture? A humidifier in winter, and/or storage in a heated room will save your wicker and rattan.

Ocassionally oiling your wicker furniture with tongue oil can lubricate and preserve it. It'll also forestall brittleness. Tongue oil can be found at almost any paint store or hardware.

Just as cold will ruin your furniture,

so will over-heating. Wicker and rattan "keep" best in moderate temperatures, as does all wood furniture. Hot dry rooms will cause your furniture to dry out and crack. Avoid placing wicker too close to fireplaces or heating units.

Many of our friends have offered a quick cover-up for scratches that appear on their walnut or mahogany furniture. They use a dab-on bottle of dark shoe polish to quickly cover the scratch. Then, they wipe over it with an extra-soft cloth to blot up any excess polish.

This tip will help you the next time you vacuum. Dampen the rollers of your upright or the brushes on your floor model with a very, very light solution of a quart of warm water and a drop or two of glycerin. You'll be surprised how much easier lint, hair, and dust picks up.

Ever wonder how to add sparkle to old plastic furniture that has lost its shine? Wonder no more. Any automotive polish or wax will make your plastics shine, and it will give them a harder surface. In a real pinch, a little toothpaste, baking soda, and a small amount of mineral water, applied with a coarse cloth will work wonders.

When dying slip-covers, here's how to set the dye. A little sea salt in the dye will help to make the color "fast" and will also deepen it. Loosely woven fabrics and fabrics that are made of natural fibers take dyes more easily and evenly than synthetics or synthetic blends.

Leather furniture can be easily cleaned. Just use any saddle soap, which you can pick up at a saddlery or shoe-repair. Use a cloth dampened with lukewarm water to apply it. Saddle soap will not clean leather furniture, but it will protect it from water and help keep it supple.

Here's a wonderful household use for old teabags. Take a week's worth of old tea-bags and boil them to get a mild tea-solution. Let it cool until luke-warm, remove the tea bags and use it to scrub your hard-wood floors and woodwork. Not only will it deep clean the surface, but it will ready it for waxing or polishing.

Remember that piano hammers are wrapped in felt. That means they make a tempting target for moths. The expense of repairing that kind of damage can be considerable. To safeguard against it, just sprinkle some moth crystals inside your piano.

If you have chairs with leather seats, here's a quick-care tip. Lemon oil will clean and condition your chair seats. Just rub it on with a soft cloth, leave it for a few minutes and rub it off. You can then shine the seat, if desired, with a rag dampened in white vinegar.

What to use to dry your dishes. As far as dish drying goes, there is no substitute for purity. Synthetic towels do not absorb. Cotton or terry leave lint. Only linen hand towels are both highly absorbent and leave no lint. Although they may cost more, your satisfaction will be worth it.

Ever wondered how to avoid a lumpy mattress? Simple, just turn your mattress once a week. Not only will you avoid lumps and sleep better, but you'll increase the "life" of your mattress.

Here's a way to clean long thin vases and jars. Vinegar, detergent, and hot water should be poured in, staying about two and one-half inches from the top. Next, add about twenty metal bee-bees, the kind used in a child's Bee-Bee gun. Place your hand over the opening and shake vigorously. The Bee-Bee's will loosen any dirt or "gunk" that has collected in the bottom. The vinegar will add sparkle to the glass.

Here's a tip to keep your aluminum pots and pans shining. Aluminum tends to dull after repeated washings with detergents, and scrubbing compounds. Lemon juice and mineral water will bring back that missing shine.

Have your ash-trays become gummed up with charred resins and tars? Denatured alcohol will clean out those smelly stains in a jiffy. It will also leave your ashtrays squeaky clean. If they are glass, a little warm water and white vinegar afterwards will make them sparkle.

Do you keep snagging your good clothes on your furniture? Don't be afraid to take a little fine-grain sandpaper to the rough area. Sand very lightly, just until the rough area disappears and then coat it with some clear nail polish. You'll never snag your lovely clothes again.

Thinking of throwing your old awnings away because they're faded and dingy? Well don't! Simply go to your local paint supply store and buy a gallon of canvas paint. Your awnings will look new again in no time.

Here's a time-saving hint. Before you move your heavy furniture again, try putting "shoes" on the pieces. Wrap old plastic dry-cleaning bags around and under the pieces' legs, so that you can move them for cleaning by yourself without marring the floors.

Want a cheap, effective cotton upholstery cleaner? Try a can of very foamy, inexpensive shaving cream! It'll lift the grime and even simple stains.

Have you ever accidentally set a hot plate or cup on a table and left a ring? If you have, I'm sure you've had the sickening feeling that you'll have to refinish to get the ring out. Not so! Try rubbing a little wax into the ring, and covering the wax with paper toweling. "Iron" the toweling with a warm iron and watch as the wax comes up, because so will the ring.

Did you know that soap film can "rot" your shower curtain? It's probably best to clean it thoroughly after each useage, but who has the time? Instead, try cleaning every two weeks or so. Just remove the hooks, laying the curtain in your tub. Scrub it with a solution of sudsy ammonia water. You can even use the shower to rinse it! After rinsing, simply hang it again to dry.

Are there "bare" places on your old mirrors? If so, you've probably just let them go because of the considerable expense of re-silvering. Well, if your bare spots are small enough, consider spraying them with silver metallic auto paint. Spray a thin coating a couple of times and then spray some clear shellac over it to seal the paint.

How do you wash your feather pillows? Instead of sending them to the cleaners, which can really be expensive, try washing them at home. Just make sure all of the ticking is in good shape first. Wash the pillow(s) on a gentle cycle, and dry them at a low heat, gentle cycle, preferably fluff. You'll be pleasantly surprised at how beautiful they emerge from your laundry.

Ever wonder how to keep your bathroom mirror from fogging? Well, no approach is actually fool-proof, but we've got a good suggestion for you. Try spraying the mirror with a mild solution of soapy, lukewarm water. Don't rinse. Instead, just let it dry partially and finish drying it with newspaper. It'll shine, and stay relatively fog-free.

Never stack your glasses. If you do stack them, chances are good that they'll get stuck. Most people break or chip glasses trying to get them unstuck. Remember, don't try to force them apart. Instead, fill the top glass with cool to cold water and then dip the glasses in a shallow pan of hot water. You'll find they come apart easily, with little or no effort.

Parchment shades can be washed. The secret is to coat them, when new, with a thin, sprayed film of flat, clear, non-yellowing shellac. Afterwards, you can wash them whenever necessary with a damp cloth.

Have you ever noticed how tired your hand gets after a day of cleaning with a scrub brush? Well, we certainly have. Your floors may be spotless, but your hand may be stiff, or ache for days because of gripping the scrub brush. We solved this problem by attaching a U-shaped door-pall to the top of the brush. It gives a better grip, and one your hand is more accustomed to.

Are you wondering how to clean brass that has become tarnished without endless scrubbing? A liberal bath in lemon juice and sea salt will. Even a soaking in the solution will easily get off all grime, tarnish, and corrosion. This idea will work for copper pots, pans, and collectables. We've also got an extra hint: once brassware is cleaned up, you might consider shellacing it. You'll never have to worry about polishing it again.

Do your glasses shine? If not, try adding a little borax to the wash water. You'll be shocked, pleasantly, at how they sparkle afterwards.

Ever wonder how "they" get window cleaner blue? Well, the answer is deceptively simple. Simple food coloring adds that blue tint you probably always thought cleaned your windows so well. As a matter of fact, we have a simple "recipe" for a similar and just as effective product. Buy an ordinary spray bottle and mix into it several liberal tablespoons of non-sudsing ammonia, a heaping tablespoon of white vinegar and a little blue food coloring. Presto, all you need now are some dirty windows!

Do you have crayon marks on your walls? What household with small children hasn't. Instead of scrubbing and scrubbing to remove them, and only succeeding in pushing them farther into the paint, try this.

Dampen a stiff, woolen cloth and pour on ordinary baking soda. Don't rub vigorously. Instead rub gently and firmly in one direction until the stain "lifts".

You can "heal" cracks in irreplaceable old china. A favorite aunt suggested this very helpful tip and we're happy to pass it along. She suggested placing the cracked china in a large pan and covering it with solution of milk and sugar. The milk should be very sweet. Slowly bring the milk and dishes to a slow, rolling boil over a low flame for 45 minutes or so. It will harden the china and make the cracks miracuously "heal".

If the backs of your mirrors are exposed, protect them. Spray shellac or varnish (clear always) will coat them and keep them from getting nicked or scratched and taking off the silver.

Never scour your dishes. If you have a particularly difficult stain or dried-on food, let it soak in a solution of hot water and baking soda. After they've soaked for twenty minutes or so, use a soft cloth and rub in a circular motion with sea salt. Your stain will lift almost immediately.

You can easily clean your blackened fireplace without scrubbing. Make a thick paste of lemon juice and soda, and leave on bricks or stone for about twenty minutes. Go over the fireplace with a damp sponge and brush lightly with stiff bristles, and you'll find the stonework clean as when it was new. You can replace the soda with pumice, if the bricks or stonework are particularly stained.

Save your woodwork and walls. If you're like us, you probably hate the gouges and scrapes that chairs and couches leave on walls, and woodwork. There is a cheap and efficient way of dealing with the problem without significantly altering your furniture or constantly re-painting your woodwork. Run lengths of 1½ inch wood quarter-round around the bottom of your woodwork, where it meets the floor. It can be stained to match your woodwork and it will easily keep your furniture away from the walls.

Do you have holes in your apartment walls where previous tenants have botched a picture hanging job? We've probably all faced this dilemma at one time or another. Here are a couple of quick, inexpensive solutions. Mix a paste of your wall paint and a little dry plaster-of-paris. You can spoon it into the cracks or holes and keep from re-painting.

If you are planning on painting anyway, try filling small holes and cracks with ordinary toothpaste. Let it dry at least a day before painting.

Here's one I bet you've never considered. **Try painting your kitchen woodwork with fabric starch.** Just make a light solution of starch and water, and use a soft brush to paint it onto your woodwork. Use a soft, damp cloth rinsed in clear warm water to rinse the woodwork after the starch has dried. When the starch comes off, so will smoke, grease, grime and food stains.

Do you have linoleum floors? Never make the mistake of varnishing them. Instead, use a no build-up wax. When you clean your floors just damp mop with a light solution of non-rinsing floor detergent and save time and money. You'll still get a clean floor!

If you're repairing your plaster walls, here's a great tip. Before you start plastering, fill the cracks with sawdust or wadded newspaper. You'll find that it takes a lot less plaster, and a lot less work.

If you use real sponges (instead of synthetic ones) here's a quick tip for keeping them long-lasting. Every two weeks or so, soak them in very cold water heavily mixed with salt. You'll double their life. After all, they came from sea water.

Are you tired of your wallpaper? Want to take it down? If you're like us, you probably want to do it yourself, but have no idea how. We decided to ask a professional painter, and this is what we found out. You make a solution from white vinegar, and clear, hot water that will loosen your wallpaper and make it easy to take down. For speed, use a roller and roll the liquid on two or three times; the paper will peel off easily.

Hate the smell of mothballs? Try using cloves, instead. The odor is invigorating and fresh, and they work every bit as good as mothballs. Just place them in cheese-cloth spice bags and hang them in closets and slip the bags into the pockets of garments while they hang.

You are only a part of the cleaning process: your tools are important. Brooms and mops left resting on their bristles and heads will wear out sooner. Instead, use a clipboard for storage, so that the mops, brooms, and sponge mops are elevated off the floor.

Are you storing or sending breakable items? Try packing delicate items in boxes filled with pop-corn and tightly seal them. It's shock-absorbing and makes a great packing material, not to mention that it is economical!

Are you afraid to wash your lampshades? Of course, the colors could run, but more likely, if you use a damp sponge and don't soak them, you'll be all right. However, to be doubly safe, train a hair-dryer on medium speed on the shade as you wash it to prevent running.

You can make your own spot remover.
Simple blend rubbing alcohol and spring
water in a ratio of two parts water to one of
alcohol. Shake them together into a squeeze
bottle and you've saved a considerable
amount of money.

**Tired of repainting your window sills
constantly?** Water and dirt can be two major reasons why you'll be repainting your
sills when the rest of your woodwork is still
in good shape. However, here's a solution.
Keep your windowsills clean with a coat of
regular floor wax. It's water resistant, and
you can wash dirt off in a hurry.

Are your blinds dingy? Even after you
wash venetian blinds, they may still look
grungy. Chances are it's the old tapes, which
may even look worse next to the newly
washed slats. Polish those tapes with a light
coating of white shoe polish. They'll look
good as new in no time.

**Ever wonder how to effectively get rid
of those ugly rings in your bath-tub?** Try
scrubbing lightly with a stiff brush and a
small amount of kerosene. Your problem
rings will go right down the drain.

**Are the edges of your linoleum curling
up?** If so, you may be fretting needlessly
over what may seem to be an expensive repair. Actually, you can do it at home. All

you'll need is a spatula and a can of linoleum cement. Just hold up the edges of the loose flooring and smear on the paste with the spatula. Pile heavy weights on the linoleum for 1 or 2 days, until the cement has set and dried thoroughly.

Quick Hints:

White vinegar, poured into your rinse cycle will eliminate lint from your wash.

If your water pipes freeze and you have no torch, try a heating pad and a hair dryer to thaw them.

A quick bath in tepid salt water will keep wicker from darkening.

To remove scratches on walnut furniture, actually rub with the shelled meat of a walnut.

Old nylon stockings make great dust cloths.

If your floors are scratched, try "sanding" them lightly with a pad of 000 steel wool (extra fine) dunked in wax and warm water. Sanding in one direction only and with the gleam of the wood, never back and forth.

Toilet bowl cleaners make great cleaning agents for delicate glassware and vases that can't be scrubbed. Simply let them soak.

Artificial (plastic) flowers can be cleaned quite simply by throwing them into a large plastic bag partially filled with coarse salt and corn meal. Just shake.

A little vinegar in your humidifier will freshen the air in your rooms.

THE KITCHEN

By calling this section "The Kitchen", we're encompassing a very large territory. In this chapter, which we consider to be one of the most important in our book, we've assembled a collection of great hints that range from how to save money preparing meals, to secrets of achieving certain effects with food, to saving that pan you burnt the spaghetti sauce in and you thought you'd have to toss. We've also collected a wealth of extremely helpful hints about caring for your utensils and a lot of nifty tips for saving time. Time and money, of course, are two of the prime considerations in the hectic world of America in the 1980's. If you're like us, you want to provide your family with the best possible meals and still stick to your budget. Added to that, of course, is a desire to no longer be a slave to kitchen ritual and endless clean-up time. In this chapter, we aim to show you how.

FOOD:

Have you ever slaved over a new and exotic dish, or even an old favorite, only to have it ruined by too much salt? Actually, it needn't be ruined at all. Try adding an apple, sliced into strips. Just remove it before serving. The apple will soak up the excess salt. <u>That goes for burned sauces and foods, too</u>.

Do you love baked potatoes, but tire of the long amount of baking time? Try boiling them first, for 5 - 7 minutes, and then wrapping them in aluminum foil and popping them into a 400 degree oven.

You don't have to cry when you chop onions. Simply chop or peel under (or close to) cold running water.

Contrary to popular opinion, once tomatoes have been picked, you shouldn't put them in sunlight. Once they are off the vine, allow them to ripen out of direct sunlight. Sunshine will only make them mushy and warm, not ripe.

Do you know how to keep your frying pan grease from splattering? Easy, just add a little salt to the cold oil or grease before you place the pan on the heat.

Does your catsup lose the race? Most thick sauces and catsups don't leave their bottles quickly because air cannot get to the bottom of the bottle. Try inserting a single chopstick all the way to the bottom and then removing it. Your catsup will flow easily.

Want a good cup of coffee? Just put a tiny pinch of salt and some egg shells in the grinds. Your coffee will be less bitter, and fresher tasting.

Hard boiled eggs may not seem like a problem, but . . . you'd be surprised at how many of our friends can't make "perfect" hard-boiled eggs. Here's our secret: we add a little white vinegar to the water. If the shells should crack while boiling, the vinegar keeps them in their shells.

Fluffier omelets are no secret. Just add a dash of cold water, a couple of dashes of skim milk, and a smidgeon of corn starch. Your omelets will be light, airy and fluffy.

Is your gravy lumpy? Here's our answer. We keep a solution of flour, water and a pinch of cornstarch, mixed to a smooth paste in the refrigerator. Just shake before using, and add slowly to warm drippings. There won't be a lump in sight.

Perfect whipped cream is no mystery. Simply chill the beaters and bowl for two or three hours (thoroughly) before using them.

If you want your jello molds to chill faster, try this: Set the mold in a pan of ice-cubes before refrigerating. It'll cut your refrigeration time in half.

Here's one you may have missed. Various relatives, great cooks all, have suggested this quick and sure-fire method for skimming the fat from home-made soup. Just wrap a few ice-cubes in cheese-cloth and dip it quickly into the soup. The fat will cling to the bag and your soup will be fat-free.

Poached eggs are a cinch. To keep the whites from spreading when you're poaching, just add a few drops of white vinegar to the water. It won't change the flavour and your eggs will be perfect.

Here's a great suggestion for left-over vegetables. At today's prices, it almost seems a sin to throw away left-over veggies. We all know, however, that re-heated fresh vegetables can turn to mush or lose their flavour the following day. Instead, try adding them as a top layer to a macaromi and cheese casserole. They'll add interest and flavour, and cut the costs of your next meal.

Did you know . . . that potatoes will take food stains off of your fingers after your food preparations? Just slice and rub a raw potato on the stain and rinse in clear-cool water.

When you clean fresh beets, don't throw away the tops. Not only are they the tastiest part of the beet, but they are the part highest in nutritional value.

Quick tips for fish:

Always bake, grill, or broil a whole fish with its head on. If it bothers you, you can remove it before serving. The presence of the head locks in moisture and freshness.

After cleaning freshly caught fish, rinse them by dunking in a pan of cold water. Don't rinse them under running water; you'll rinse away the flavour, too.

When broiling whole fish, turn it only **once.** Cook thoroughly on one side and then turn and cook on the other. (Brushed-on, generous amount of butter and lemon juice will only enhance the flavour).

The color of the chicken's skin is important when buying. White skin, or skin that easily shows the chicken veins is not a sign of good poultry. The skin should be plump and colored a creamy yellow to get the finest flavour.

Bored with the same old meat and potatoes? Well, for variety's sake, try some of what we call the "forgotten" meats. Kidneys, liver, tongue, hearts, even brains can be fixed in a number of tasty and interesting ways. They'll also be easier on your tight budget.

Ever considered soybeans? As a meat extender, that is. Cooked soybeans make a great extender for ground beef in meat loaf, and the taste and texture approximate that of meat. How's that for a budgeting tip?

The next time you make gravy, here's a nice twist. Try mixing the flour you'll be using with instant potato granules. You'll be shocked at the flavour boost!

Does your stored sugar harden into a large "rock"? Just place a slice of soft white bread in the bag with it, close it up and leave for a couple of hours. When you open it, it'll be granulated again.

Stale crackers and chips can be revived. Just heat them on a cookie sheet in a hot oven or under a hot broiler.

Ever wonder why some people's rice is perfect while yours is sticky, or stays in clumps? The answer is really quite simple. Undoubtedly, they added about a teaspoon of fresh lemon juice to the water before boiling.

You can help cut fruit from browning. Just spray cut fruit with a little fresh lemon juice or toss them with lemon juice in a bowl. It won't change the flavour noticeably, but it will help them from turning brown.

Cut the cooking time for hamburgers in half. Make several holes in the center of each patty and the inside will cook about twice as fast.

How can you tell if your eggs have "gone bad"? A bad egg will float in cool water, while a fresh, useable one will immediately sink to the bottom.

Ever wonder how restaurants keep their bacon from curling? They dip the bacon in ice-cold water before frying, and the edges won't curl.

Should honey be thrown away once it has "sugared"? Certainly not! Simply boil the jar in a pan of water, and the honey will return to its original state.

Get more juice out of your lemons. Several of our friends tell us that fresh lemons give almost twice as much juice if they are covered (in a pan) with hot water for about 20 minutes before squeezing.

Many chefs have told us an easy way for removing the core from lettuce. Simply smack the core end against your countertop and it will pop right out. This insures that the browning and metallic taste that results from cutting with a knife don't happen.

Mix in powdered milk instead of fresh when making mashed potatoes. Not only will you save money, but you'll find your potatoes are firmer and less liquidy.

Here's a quick method for "freshening" slightly stale bread or rolls. Wrap the bread or rolls in dampened paper towels and place them inside a regular brown bag. Place them in a 350 degree oven for 3 - 4 minutes.

Salt can easily draw moisture and clog your shakers. To prevent this, add a few grains of rice to keep it from clogging.

Line your broiler pan with aluminum foil. It'll cut down on your clean-up time considerably. You may also want to fill it with a little water to absorb smoke and spatters. A favorite aunt relayed that a large piece of French bread diced in the broiler pan will soak up the grease from cooking lamb or pork and cut the cleaning time considerably.

Make your hamburgers beautiful and tasty. If your family is tired of the same old burgers, try this. Saute onions and sliced mushrooms (just a handful) and then mix them into the uncooked hamburger. To make them lovely and equal, use an ice-cream scoop to measure out each patty. Flatten and fry these treats for your family.

Here's the quick way to thaw chicken. Run cold water over frozen chicken until it becomes malleable. Be careful to make sure that the poultry is not allowed to stand in water because it will soak out the flavours.

The next time you roast a chicken, try this. If your chicken dries out when you roast it, just place an apple, whole, inside the chicken. The apple will keep the chicken moist and tender. Throw the apple away when the chicken is finished roasting.

Can you tell if fish is fresh? Although most people can't tell, there are a number of easy indicators to help you gauge the freshness of seafood and freshwater fish.

The odor is probably the first thing that comes to mind, although you may be surprised to know that many people associate a foul, fishy odor with all fish.

If that smell is above a subtle whiff, it indicates the fish has been stored for a while. If it is bothersomely strong, it probably means the fish is bad.

The skin of a fresh fish is colorful and shiny. Old fish is grayed-out, or faded.

Redness in the gills is an easy sign of freshness. If the gills have turned a brownish-gray, buy elsewhere!

Although most fish buyers in supermarkets and fish stalls overlook them, the eyes are an important indicator. They should protrude and have a healthy transparency. Stale or old fish have sunken, cloudy eyes; avoid them.

Different vegetables are best stored different ways. Although it's best to eat fresh corn on the cob the day you buy it, it's not always practical. If you must store it longer, be sure to leave all the outside leaves on. Wrap the ears in damp cotton kitchen towels and refrigerate.

Always clip the "tops" of vegetables like parsnips, carrots, beets and turnips. The leafy tops will use the moisture of the edible part of the vegetable and dry them out.

Peas and beans, squash and cucumbers, and even tomatoes store best in the refrigerator just as they are.

When buying oysters, clams, and

mussels, check the shell. These shellfish should always be alive in the shell before eating and the shells should be whole and closed tightly.

Quick tips for food:

Cauliflower steamed with a lemon wedge will be whiter and less bitter.

Always remember that vegetables lose their vitamins and minerals if they are overcooked. Cooked veggies should be crisp and crunchy.

Beets will peel much more easily if dumped in cold , clear water after boiling.

Cooking shears or ordinary household sessions can be a real timesaver in the kitchen.

Young, fresh vegetables are lower in starch content and tastier.

Once frozen fish is thawed, **do not** refreeze it.

Sea-scallops are larger and cheaper than bay scallops, and both have a sweet taste and firm texture.

Lobsters should always be bought alive, and showing movement.

If you're perplexed at how much meat to buy for each family member, a good rate of thumb is $1/3$ to $1/2$ pound of boneless meats for person. Go a little heavier for boned meats. Base your decision on the size of the bones.

To keep your gravy dark, brown the flour first.

If your gravy is a little greasy, try adding a pinch of soda.

A clean nail shoved into your baked potato will lessen the cooking time by twelve to fifteen minutes.

To make your new frying pan stickless, try boiling a little apple cider vinegar in it.

Vinegar is also a natural odor absorber. An open bowl in your kitchen while cooking will soak your smells and smoke.

Before you measure a cup of honey, wipe the measuring cup with oil and rinse it out with boiling water. The honey won't stick.

To keep your sausages from shrinking, just boil them for a few minutes before frying.

Pierce the shell of an egg with a pinpoint before plunging into boiling water and the shell won't break.

Garlic cloves stored in a little olive oil will last forever.

Cheese can be kept moist and fresh longer by soaking a little cheese-cloth in white wine vinegar and wrapping in it.

Marshmallows can stay fresh for an indefinite length of time when frozen.

All salad greens keep better in paper bags in your refrigerator than in plastic. The paper breathes and doesn't trap dampness.

Line the vegetable drawer with toweling . . . either paper or cotton. It'll absorb the moisture and your veggies will keep longer.

To insure that all your popcorn pops, rinse it in ice water.

You can combine salt and pepper in a large shaker for use during cooking: it'll save time and effort.

TIME SAVERS

The next time you use your blender and it's time for clean-up, don't. Instead, pour hot water and a little dish-washing liquid in and set the blender on puree. It'll be clean in seconds.

Are your appliances in working order, but stained from food? Try scrubbing it with a little inexpensive baking soda. They'll shine in no time, and many of the stains will disappear, too.

Is your old tooth-brush worn out? Well, don't throw it away. Old toothbrushes make great scrubbing tools for the kitchen. You'll find them to be invaluable time-savers when it comes to cleaning egg-beaters, in particular.

Are your good china cups stained with coffee or tea? Once more, good old reliable baking soda is your answer! Just put about half a teaspoon and some hot water in each cup and let them soak. Scrub lightly with a soft cloth and rinse; your stains will be gone.

Does your garbage disposal have an unpleasant odor? Ours did, but a helpful neighbor suggested this easy method for sweetening it up. After you've eaten an orange, grapefruit or squeezed lemons, just feed the rinds into the disposal. It'll freshen the air and eliminate any unpleasant smells.

Don't throw away those nicked or scratched drinking glasses. If they're nicked on the rim, try filing them slightly with an extra fine emery board. You'll be amazed at just how well it works.

Boil a solution of vinegar and water in your teakettle occasionally. All teakettles, pots, pans, in fact, anything you boil water in a lot, build up a mineral deposit that can change the taste of whatever you're making.

A mild solution of one part white wine vinegar to two parts spring water, slow boiled in the container(s) occasionally will alleviate this problem, without time-consuming scrubbing.

Ever wonder how much a pound of butter is in cups? Well, so have we. Many recipes call for so many cups, half cups, etc. of butter. We buy butter, however, by the stick or pound, and that can be confusing. Simply remember this: there are four sticks of butter to a pound, and one pound of butter is two cups. Simple subtraction or addition will save you time-consuming measurements when you're cooking or baking.

How many measuring cups do you have? Or measuring spoons, for that matter? Always keep at least **two** measuring cups handy while cooking or baking: one for dry ingredients, and one for oily or liquid things. You won't have to take time during preparation to clean out a measuring cup. It goes the same way with measuring spoons, too.

Here's one you may have overlooked. Did you know that you can freeze cakes? It's actually a real time saver! You can bake your cakes a few days ahead of time, freeze them, and thus eliminate last minute baking. You won't feel as rushed before your parties and gatherings.

If your recipe calls for melted chocolate, here's an easy tip. Just grease the pan you'll use for melting first. It'll save time afterwards during clean-up.

Always remember to use cold water when making gravy. Hot water may make lumps. Cold water will save you time and the frustration of trying to beat-out those bothersome lumps.

You can freeze fried chicken. Although it has been our experience that most fried foods do not freeze well, fried chicken is the exception. You can freeze it for those unexpected drop-ins or last minute invitations. Once thawed, you can eat it hot or cold; it's perfect for emergencies or those days you just don't want to cook!

No dessert? Don't forget the stale cake! We know, you're probably thinking, are they crazy? Well, stale cake can make a great quick fresh dessert in just seconds. Wrap the cake in a damp, lint-less piece of cloth (linen or cheese-cloth) and place in a warm oven. The moisture from the cloth will "steam" the cake, and freshen it. Then, try a little warmed apricot jam to give it a distinctive flavour.

Where do you store your sugar? Try keeping it in the refrigerator. Both brown and refined sugars keep better and will not harden. The moist cold of the refrigerator keeps them granulated. You'll save time and effort when you're baking.

Ever wonder how to measure molasses without gumming up the measuring cup? Molasses can take forever to roll back out of a measuring cup. Unless, of course, you try this hint: fill your cup first with fine, white flour. Dump all the flour back out and pour in the molasses. It'll easily pour back out and save you a load of clean-up time.

Here's how to peel tomatoes in a hurry. Put your tomatoes in the refrigerator for two or three hours, or until they're chilled thoroughly. Remember, **do not** freeze them. Run the blunt edge of a table knife over them, top to bottom, completely around. Take a sharper knife and pierce the skin. The tomato will peel effortlessly and quickly.

If you use an electric frying pan, here's a quick tip to remember. Prop up one or two legs (if two, make sure they're both on the same side) slightly. The excess grease from whatever you're frying will run to one end, alleviating the necessity of draining and thereby saving you time.

This is a sure cure for tough meat. If you're like us, you probably hate to tenderize meat with a meat hammer. Instead, if you've purchased a cheaper, tougher grade of meat, try tenderizing our way. Simply make a marinade of one part white vinegar to two parts beef broth and marinate the meat for two to two and a half hours before cooking. Simply drain, pat dry with paper toweling and you'll have a tender piece of meat.

Would you like to save time shucking clams and oysters? It's easy! About one hour before you plan on cooking them, soak them in ice-water, and after you've drained them, place them in a plastic bag and place in your freezer. After you take them out, rap with the handle of a kitchen knife, and they'll ease open.

Does your recipe call for melted butter, but you've forgotten to set it out ahead? Don't worry! Just grate it with an ordinary cheese grater and it'll melt quickly.

Ever wonder if there is an easy, fast way to get corn silk off of a fresh ear of corn? Well, quit wondering, because there is. Just run a damp paper napkin lengthwise down an ear of corn and the silks will cling to the paper. How's that for quick and easy?

Want to avoid scrubbing off burned food? If you've ever burned food onto a favorite pot or pan, you've probably experienced the frustration and endless time involved in trying to scrub it clean. Instead of using your time and elbow-grease, try this method we've "cooked" up. Heat the pan on the top of the stove until it is fairly warm all through. Scatter a mixture of dry Clorox and dry detergent over the burned-on food and cover it with paper toweling soaked in hot water. Leave it for twenty minutes to an hour depending on how badly burned on the food is. Rinse and wash as your normally would, and your pan will come clean.

Hate to polish copper? Here's the quick way to clean them and keep them beautiful. Mix a little vinegar and salt in a shallow dish. Cut a lemon in half and dip it in the mixture. Work the cut surface of the lemon in a circular motion on the copper. It's not necessary to rub hard. Rinse the pan in lukewarm water and dry. You'll admire the fresh-scrubbed shine.

Don't use your valuable time scrubbing the kitchen sink. Instead, soak a few paper towels in ordinary bleach and leave them in the sink overnight. You'll be pleasantly surprised in the morning.

Want to cut your defrosting time? The next time you defrost your refrigerator-freezer, do this. Wipe the sides of the freezer (and the bottom and top) with a cloth dampened in a solution of glycerin and water. You'll find that ice and frost will easily and quickly lift off.

Quick hints:

A warm butter knife is the quickest way to loosen a cooking or baking mold.

A hot knife is the best way to cut anything sticky when baking. It'll also save on clean-up time, as almost nothing sticks to a heated blade.

To keep your meat loaf from sticking to the pan, and cut clean-up time, put a strip of bacon on the bottom of the dish before putting in the loaf.

Sharp knives will cut your preparation time considerably.

If you're going to freeze a cake, don't frost it. Most frosting can be stored in the refrigerator for several days before using, but most don't freeze well.

If you're storing a fruit cake, here's a quick hint for freshening it before serving: wrap in cheese-cloth soaked in rum or brandy and place in a warm oven for 10 minutes.

Don't thaw foods until the day you eat them. It may save time, but it'll cut down on flavour.

A little cheese-cloth around the end of a lemon before you squeeze will save your searching for seeds later.

A lemon stored in water will keep longer, and yield more juice with less squeezing.

To thaw frozen fruit or berries quickly, put the box or bag in a zip-lock plastic bag and let stand in warm water for twenty minutes.

Freezing food ahead for the week's meals is a real time saver.

Organize your shelves, refrigerator, cupboard and freezer. You'll find that in the long run you'll save loads of time cooking and cleaning.

Try making an inventory of kitchen cooking items. It'll cut down shopping time.

If you do home-canning, always label. It'll save you time when you need something later.

Divide large food items into servings before freezing. Cooking will take less time and you'll find you only cook what you need.

A hair-dryer is a quick aid in defrosting.

A little apple juice boiled with a dull aluminum pan is the quickest way to restore the shine.

Never scour glass baking dishes. You'll save time and effort and not scratch up the pan by using an old lemon half, instead.

Wax kitchen shelves, and you'll save cleaning time. They'll come clean with just a damp cloth.

Save time in the morning by organizing your kitchen the night before. You can even go so far as setting the table or pre-cooking bacon.

Refrigerated candles won't drip and cause clean-up headaches after your next big dinner.

A few raw potatoes added to water containing wilted greens will quickly perk them up.

Save clean-up time by preventing boil-overs. Just add a few drops of olive oil to boiling water to prevent this.

A double thickness of paper toweling makes a quick replacement for coffee filters when you accidentally run short.

You'll find a small plastic funnel, lightly greased will be an invaluable kitchen aid, and it'll clean quickly, too.

Rubbing alcohol makes a quick, cheap kitchen utensil clean-up agent.

Before you wash your meat-grinder, try grinding stale bread through it. You'll find it cleans much more quickly.

Ammonia straight from the bottle makes a fast, inexpensive oven cleaner.

SPICING UP YOUR COOKING

Many of us are just plain cautious when it comes to the use of spices in our cooking. Just exactly why that is, is hard to say. I've a feeling, though, that it's a caution that's handed down, and for no good reason.

We tend to forget, that the discovery of the new world was really centered around finding a cheaper way to bring back spices from India and China; that's how precious our ancestors thought them to be! Most of us, however, know very little about when to use them, how much to use, and what spices to use with which foods. Consequently, we've included this chapter to help you get acquainted with this huge body of kitchen helpers. As you've probably guessed, we feel that the addition of great spices can be the difference between a budget meal and a great (budget) meal! Just because money is tight, is no reason to assume that meals should be bland or uninteresting. Be adventurous! Spices are a great way to liven up those tired old recipes and bring smiles to the faces of your family at meal-time.

When we say spices, which ones come instantly to mind? If you're like most of us, you'll jump right in with "salt" and "pepper", and perhaps even offer "cinnamon" or "garlic". After that, however, you'll begin to falter. Because most of us don't have a working knowledge of spices, their names, and what they're used for and with, we've decided to list them for you and then tell you what each is best with.

Cloves: whole cloves are great with pork, and add a special zing to ham. Try studding a whole ham with them before you bake it the next time. Cloves will also liven up yellow vegetables, and are great in the fall with butter nut squash; try a little cinnamon with the squash, too!

Tarragon: the next time you make chicken salad, don't just throw in a little mayonnaise and some salt; add a dash of ground-up tarragon and see what a difference it makes. Add some to salad dressings and see how much they perk up. Be sure to add some whole leaves to bottles of white vinegar, and taste the flavor difference.

Allspice: this spice is exactly what the name implies. It'll liven up any vegetable from black-eyed peas and baked beans to summer squash. Throw a little on baked apples and you'll savor their aroma through the whole house.

Fennel: fennel, whole seeds or crushed, tastes like a sophisticated version of licorice. You'll be pleasantly surprised how it livens up shrimp creole, fish chowders, stuffed crab, and other seafood dishes. Baked chicken has never suffered from the addition of fennel, and many coffee cake recipes come to life with a little fennel thrown in.

Nutmeg: many recipes call for nutmeg when making puddings, cakes, pies, and cookies, but it can be added to other things, too. Try it sprinkled on creamed spinach. Or creamed corn. You'll find it changes the flavor completely. The next time you make hot chocolate, add a little nutmeg and some cinnamon; it's a great addition to after-dinner coffee, too.

Mint: most people think of mint only in association with tea. Other nations, however, use it to add a delicate flavor to lamb and to spice sauces for roast beef and pork. The next time you make a roast for your family, try adding mint to the carrots, onions and potatoes you always pile around the meat. You'll be impressed with the flavor change.

Curry: This spice is not actually one spice at all, but a fabulous mixture of about two dozen spices that include ginger, cumin, cloves, and peppers. This Indian taste treat is, of course, hot, and should be used with the appropriate amount of respect unless you like your food spicey and are used to it. Curry is a great addition to almost any meat, fowl, fish or vegetable dish, but we really find it livens up fish dishes the most.

Cardamon: this spice is best used in association with other spices. Try it with anything you'd normally use nutmeg or cinnamon or both with. It's also great for making spiced ice coffee.

Saffron: this is the Rolls-Royce of spices. Incredibly expensive, saffron adds a distinctive, unforgettable flavor to rice and/or curry dishes, and a distinctive yellow coloring, too. It also works wonders on chicken, shrimp, crab, and lobster dishes.

Tumeric: while not nearly as expensive as saffron, this spice adds a similar coloration and the approximate flavor. Try it, like saffron, with rice, seafood, and chicken. It especially adds zest to home-made chicken pot-pies.

Garlic: we could write a whole book about garlic, and we're sure someone already has. This distinctive spice should not be confined merely to Italian cooking, because it's great with practically everything. That's not to say that it doesn't perk up pastas, or add interest to red or white sauces, but its also a great addition to fried chicken. Try it with practically any soup, and garlic butter will make any bread or roll better. Fish soups are especially complemented by its addition, and no vegetable ever suffered from a sprinkle or two of garlic salt.

Bay leaves: friends have commented that the bay leaf can turn even the dullest soups into winners. Its addition to home-made, or even canned soups, enhances the flavors tremendously. Gravies, seafood soups, and roasts are enlivened by the simple bay leaf, too.

Coriander: this ancient, lemon-like flavored spice adds a pleasant oomph to almost all baked goods. Try it with pies, cookies, cakes, and dessert breads. Biscuits and home-made crackers will even benefit by its presence. It's also great with salad greens, and cold garden vegetables.

Marjoram: any Italian dish is sparked by a sprinkle of marjoram, especially Italian fish dishes. Try a little on home-made bread sticks, too.

Rosemary: along with parsley, sage and thyme, this is probably the best known "exotic" spice. Still, few people use it as much as they should. Try adding its delicate flavors to roast chicken, or creamy chicken salad. Crush it and add it to oil and vinegar for a tasty salad dressing. Try it with olive oil, thyme, and garlic as a marinade for sliced tomatoes, or as a topping for par-boiled green beans, carrots, and onion. A little in any soups will help the flavors immensely. Try it with lamb and veal.

Oregano: this is the best spice for tomatoes. The Italians sprinkle it liberally on sliced tomatoes and add a little oil for a simple, delicious salad. Oregano is also a great "rub" for pork or veal roasts, and is a must for great potato salads.

Thyme: this is an all-purpose spice. Try this delightful, aromatic herb with all kinds of stuffings, stews, or old-fashioned yankee pot roasts. It'll add zing to any vegetable when you add it to melted butter and pour it over them. Try it without fear on any cheese or tomato dish.

Basil: scrambled eggs will never be considered dull again after a little crushed basil is added to them. It enhances and complements the natural flavor of the egg. You'll also find that it's great in all tomato dishes and sauces, and does wonders for a salad.

Dill: this piquant spice adds flavor to anything it touches, but be sure to use it with a light hand. Baked and broiled fish dishes, fish stews and chowders, potato and vegetable salads, and all shell fish, become a treat with the addition of this spice.

Caraway: as a spice, both the leaves and the seeds of this plant are used. The seeds work wonders with breads, rolls, and marinades, while the leaves are best used to spice soups (especially those with chicken or beef in them). If you use the seed, remember to partially crush them first; it releases the flavor.

Parsley: probably the most commonly used herb, we've included it because it's such a necessity for creative cooking, especially when preparing budget meals. This spice easily blends with others, but manages to maintain its own delicate flavors. Parsley can be used with almost any dish, especially with soups, sauces, and hearty meat stews, to liven their flavors.

Capers: these tiny buds have a large, pickle-like flavor. They are great in cooked, chilled vegetable spreads, and are excellent in most sauces. They are especially tasty in sauces used for fish.

Chives: this spice, actually a form of very mild onions, may get our vote for all-around most useful spice. You can top soups with it, blend it with sour cream to make dips, sprinkle it on omelets to add zing, and add it to all butter sauces for flavor. Try some on macaroni and cheese to liven it up.

Chervil: a delicately flavored herb, it seems to really enhance chicken and other fowl. You'll also find it great on rarebits and old-fashioned savories, not to mention its usefulness on omelets and salads. Vegetables, in general, are enhanced by it.

In general, cooking with spices is nothing to be frightened of. Most spices impart a delicate, flavor-enhancing aura to your cooking, as long as you don't get too heavy-handed with them. When in doubt as to whether a spice will work, try it! Just a taste will generally tell you, and you'll be surprised how much spices can change the flavor and aroma of hum-drum or budget meals. Just because you're saving money doesn't mean you shouldn't eat as well as possible, and it certainly doesn't mean you should stop being creative in your cooking.

Quick hints:

When in doubt about using an herb, be subtle. Usually, just a little will tell you whether it's the flavor you're searching for.

In season, grown your own spices. Most will grow in pots on window ledges, and the seeds are inexpensive. Just follow directions.

When using a variety of herbs, tie them in cheese-cloth before dropping them in. They'll be easy to retrieve, and no one will get a bay leaf in his or her portion.

The same goes for roasting turkeys, chickens, or game hens.

Vanilla is a natural sweetner. Try it instead of sugar.

Always store spices in a cool, dark place. We put ours in the refrigerator.

Bay leaves, bundled, will keep insects out of your kitchen drawers.

Here's a quick way to get garlic odor off of your hands: wash with salt, baking soda, and warm water.

Before you put whole garlic cloves in a roast or dish, skewer them with toothpicks to make them easier to retrieve.

Garlic will keep indefinitely in a sealed jar filled with vegetable oil. And it won't smell-up the refrigerator, either.

You can always substitute onion salt or onion flakes for the "real" thing.

Don't buy expensive pie spices, the kind that come already blended. They are just cloves, cinnamon, ginger, and nutmeg.

The same goes for those spices called poultry spices. Blend savory, thyme, sage and marjoram and you'll have the same product, without the added cost.

A raw potato or sliced apple in too-salty soup will correct the problem.

If you get too much garlic in a dish, try filling a tea-ball with dried parsley. It'll absorb a lot of the flavor.

Fresh parsley, chewed, will also take away garlic breath.

Spices lose potency with age. They'll keep for about a year, but should be checked out regularly.

Vinegar makes a great marinade for

cheaper, tougher cuts of meat.

A little vinegar added to milk will sour it when the recipe calls for soured milk.

PACKING AND LUGGAGE

Have you traveled somewhere only to discover that once there and unpacked, you ended up ironing or washing because of your lousy packing job? Clothes, it is true, don't make the person but we all base our first reactions to people on how they look. A vacation or business trip is important enough to warrant looking good, and you can't look good if you packed badly and ruined your clothing.

Space is also a consideration. In the 1980's, there are restrictions on how much luggage you can bring onto airplanes or trains without paying extra. If you're traveling by car, space is still a consideration. As the size of the average car decreases, the amount of things we can bring along does, also. Proper packing and care of your luggage will allow you to bring the largest amount of clothing in the least amount of luggage, and everything will survive the trip in better shape.

In this chapter, we'll show a few great hints on packing, and a number of simple care instructions for your luggage.

If you are going to store your luggage for a long period of time before using again, try this: a clean piece of luggage lasts longer and will be cleaner when you do want to use it next. If you're going to store your luggage for long periods of time, don't just place them in the attic. Make cheese-cloth sachets of herbs and moth-balls to place inside each piece. Wrap the cases in brown butcher's paper to keep dirt from the surface and to keep the luggage from being marred or stained.

Don't wash the inside of your cases. Most linings are glued, not stitched. Any contact with liquid may loosen them. Clean instead with a little dusting powder and a vacuum. It'll freshen, clean, and save your linings!

Be extra careful in packing cosmetic and toiletries. Try to take only items you need in plastic, unbreakable containers. If that is not possible, make sure that glass containers are not touching. Wrap them in paper toweling and aluminum foil to cushion them against shocks and prevent spillage and breakage. More than one vacation has been ruined by broken shampoo or make-up containers.

Women, here's a hint for packing lingerie. Place the lingerie flat on a piece of tissue paper, and, starting at one end, roll into a medium tight roll. The tissue on the outside will protect it, and rolling should alleviate wrinkling. Also, the lingerie will take up less room in your suitcase.

Is your leather luggage old, dark, and dirty looking? Here's an easy, quick, and inexpensive tip to restore some of its beauty.

A little lemon oil, or a half a lemon rubbed onto leather will "bleach" it without drying it out. A coating of saddle soap afterwards will clean and polish the luggage, and bring it closer to its original coloration.

Does it really make a difference, when packing, about what-goes-where? Of course it does! You should always pack the heaviest clothing and objects first, getting lighter and lighter as you approach the top of the case. In that way, the heavier things won't crush lighter and more delicate articles.

Always try to pack shoes and hats in separate cases. Obviously, hats and shoes pack best in cases designed for their travel. All of us, however, can't afford highly specific pieces of luggage. If shoes are going in your main case with everything else, they should go in shoe bags. Old dry cleaner's plastic makes a cheap, useful wrap for shoes, or for stuffing hats to help them retain their shape.

If you're taking perfume, remember this: virtually all scent manufacturers make travel vials. Not only do they not take up as much room, but they can easily be wrapped in aluminum foil to avoid accidents.

Always pack at the last possible moment. A good rule of thumb is to see that your clothing is actually in the suitcase the shortest amount of time possible. You can always pack certain things (sweaters, shoes, belts, toiletries) as far ahead as you desire, but try not to pack dresses, coats, suits, shirts or blouses until right before leaving. If you pack ahead of time, simply leaving the suitcases open until right before leaving. Conversely, unpack as soon as you can!

Do you have fiber-glass or plastic luggage? If so, it can be cleaned with a damp sponge and a little mild detergent. Never use a bleach or harsh detergent, because plastics can fade. **If you have cloth luggage,** it can be cleaned with a stiff brush and a little ammonia. **Aluminum or steel luggage** will brighten right up by scrubbing it with a soft cloth and a little lemon juice.

Quick hints on the art of packing:

Tissue paper is an absolute necessity for packing well.

Ties should be folded in half lengthwise and then rolled with tissue paper. This will keep the tie from wrinkling.

Blouses and shirts should both be packed using the same method. Lay them, placket up, on a sheet or two of tissue paper. Fold the shoulders and sleeves behind, and then fold the body three times. A little tissue paper tucked under the collar will keep it from flattening out.

Socks, belts, hosiery, ties, and slippers should be placed closely together.

Rolling your clothing takes up less room and keeps them freer from wrinkles.

The best way to pack men's suits is in a type of suitcase called a "two-suiter". You'll find it easier to pack in, and everything will wrinkle less.

Skirts should be treated similarly to shirts. Lay a couple of pieces of tissue paper, folding each side over until they meet in the back. Place the folded skirt on more tissue and loosely roll it.

Dresses should be packed just like skirts.

Don't button or zip jackets when you pack them. Just overlap the sides.

When packing suits or sports coats, always line the body of the coat with tissue paper. Stuff the shoulders with tissue, also, so that the padding isn't ruined.

Always "ball" socks instead of folding them; they will take up less room.

STAINS

We don't need to tell you about the rising cost of dry-cleaning today. Inflation has hit everywhere, but one of the easiest areas to spot the rise is in cleaning where prices have quadrupled. Of course, one of the things that bothered us the most about this, is that many spot stains could be gotten out at home.

Many kitchen and laundry-items will effectively clean spots. Dr. Bronner's Castile Soap, vinegar, petroleum jelly, chlorine bleach, and ammonia will all get out a wide variety of stains. Old tooth-brushes and a regular, stiff brush are indispensable.

Although most fabrics can be easily cleaned at home, you should be wary of certain ones. Rayons, velvets, extremely delicate laces, and heavily flocked fabrics should be left alone. Trust them to a competent cleaner. A professional dry-cleaner will have the equipment, knowledge, and space to handle these fabrics. Also, don't tackle any jobs you're uncertain of; it's too easy to ruin your favorite clothes. Be especially wary of clothing that is not color-fast, or very intricate prints that could run. You can always test a spot on the inside seam or hem to see if your cleaning may have serious consequences. Always test before you try any cleaner on a garment: better safe than sorry. The price of dry-cleaning, no matter how high, doesn't seem quite so much when compared to the price of your clothing!

Home cleaning can be advantageous, but it can also be dangerous. Some cleaning agents are irritants, some are poisonous, and still others are flammable. Understand what you're dealing with, and as a general rule, forego using any dangerous ones. Be especially wary of alkalines. Not only are they dangerous, but they will seriously harm wools, silks, and furs, while not really bothering cotton, unless used at full strength.

Whereas alkalines should never be used on animal fibers, all acids are harmful to plant fibers. It's best to avoid their use entirely, leaving their handling to professionals.

Be careful with delicate fabrics. Silks, voilles, cotton gauzes, and jerseys do not react well to excessive scrubbing. If you must scrub them, use the softest brush you can find. Better, of course, is to work the fabric against itself. Rub gently, with a broad back-and-forth motion. When you rinse, rinse the entire garment to avoid water spotting.

It's better to work a spot two or three times sparingly, rather than to scrub it vigorously only once. "Water down" your cleaning agents, and apply them several times. Your fabrics will react better and will look better afterward. A single, full strength application and hard scrub may ruin the cloth, or, though it may lift the stain, may cause a permanent reminder of your cleaning that looks worse than the stain did.

Did you think stains on leather or suede were permanent? Well, guess again! Ordinary club soda is the best cleaning agent. Just use the soda and an old toothbrush, rubbing the stain back and forth. A suede brush should be used on the suede after the spot dries to return the flattened nap to its previous condition.

Alcohol stains set quickly, so it's necessary to act quickly when spills occur. You'll also find that they turn a yellowish-brown color as they age, which can ruin almost any garment.

Soak the stained fabric in a mild solution of water and glycerine. The glycerine will soften the stain and make it easier to lift. If you scrub the spot(s), do so very gently, and do not use a brush. Rinse in a heavier solution of clear vinegar and cold water.

White wine vinegar is one of the few things that gets chewing gum off of fabrics. An easier solution, however, may be to simply freeze the garment. Once chilled, the gum should become brittle and break or peel off the cloth.

Perhaps the most common stains on clothing are caused by perspiration. I'm sure you've had some of your favorite white or colored clothing ruined by these yellow stains just as we have. Although there is no sure-fire method for getting the stains out, we think we've come up with a winner. Before laundering, try a thirty minute pre-soak in luke-warm water heavily laced with white vinegar. You can "work" the stains with your hands, but don't scrub. After soaking, launder as you normally would.

Although you may get the stain out, how do you avoid water-staining of a garment? Professional cleaners call this kind of cleaning and drying "feathering". That means, that you avoid water-stains from appearing by making sure the edges of the wet area dry before the inner area where you lifted the spot does. An electric portable hair-dryer, used in a circular motion will help you to achieve this.

Butter can be removed easily. Many of our friends complain that butter is perhaps the hardest stain for them to remove, but this needn't be so. We recommend a two-step method for cleaning that incorporates both a wet and dry cleaning method.

With a soft, natural dry sponge apply a small amount of any grease solvent. It'll dry very, very quickly. As soon as it's dry, dampen the sponge in warm, warm water and a mild shampoo and scrub gently until the stain lifts.

Next to butter, many friends consider blood to be the most difficult stain to get out. You probably have the most efficient stain remover for this particular stain in your kitchen cabinet already! Just make a heavy paste of meat tenderizer and cold water. Apply it with a damp sponge and leave it on for twenty to thirty minutes. When it's dry, rinse it off with cold water and your stain will be gone.

Chocolate can be a toughy. There is an excellent way for removing these stains, though. Use a dry grease solvent. Apply the solvent to the chocolate, but don't brush it. Let the solvent dry. When it's dry, use fingers to work in a mild solution of dish washing detergent and warm water. Don't rinse, but go ahead and launder immediately.

Don't throw away ink-stained clothing! A little ordinary hair spray will get it out. Just spray on the aerosol and rub the spot(s) with a coarse, dry cloth. Afterwards, launder the garment as you normally would.

Ever tried to get a lipstick stain out? Well, so have we, and we've been just as frustrated as you! One local dry-cleaner suggested we try the following method. While it's not 100% effective, it's the best method we've found so far.

Smear the stain with an extra-thin coating of Vaseline; be careful not to rub the stain in the fabric, though. A Q-tip swab will do the trick. Next, pour on a liberal amount of grease solvent, and continue to flush the area with it, waiting until each application dries. After the color appears to lift, soak the garment in mild solution of warm water, two or three drops of ammonia, and a little mild shampoo; keep it soaking for about an hour. Rinse afterward in warm water and launder immediately afterward.

Mildew stains are no problem! If the cloth will stand up to it, a mild solution of ammonia and warm water used as a soak should be just what the doctor ordered!

Tea is a problem stain. Most tea stains will wash out if laundered immediately. The ones that do not present more of a problem. Of course, if the fabric is white, a little warm water, chlorine bleach, and a toothbrush will get the stain out in no time. On colored fabrics, however, it's more difficult. An extremely weak solution of hydrogen peroxide and water will usually work if flushed continuously with cold water. It's best to test the fabric first, though, because there is always the danger that it will bleed or bleach.

Lemon juice will take out rust stains. Use a sponge, apply a solution of lemon juice and sea salt. Rinse immediately afterwards with cold water and launder the garment as soon as possible.

This will get out wine stains. Ordinary household cooking salt is your best crack at getting out wine stains, especially red wine. Rinse the cloth first in cold water. Pour on a liberal amount of cooking salt and scrub vigorously with a soft toothbrush.

Tar can be easily removed with a little kerosene. Easily, that is, if you tackle it before it's been on a piece of clothing for very long. Tar is one of those stains that you'll almost certainly get out if you begin work on it quickly enough. Dip an old toothbrush in a little kerosene and rub vigorously. Dunk immediately into a hand-wash of detergent and warm water. Work the stain by scrubbing it with your hands. You can rinse it in cool water. Incidentally, only use kerosene if you're sure the fabric is color-fast.

Here's a tip for getting rid of lead pencil stains. A lead pencil can cause one of the toughest stains, because it is almost imbedded in the fiber of the cloth. We suggest working the dampened fabric with the blunt, bristleless end of your toothbrush and a solution of high strength liquid laundry detergent and a few drops of ammonia. When the stain begins to lift, flush the area with grease solvent and warm water, alternately until it's gone. Rinse the garment in cool water afterward.

This one will get rid of those dirt stains that leave you with "ring-around-

the-collar". We all know simple scrubbing won't take out those rings, but a neighbor of ours suggested this. Take a stick of white chalk, the kind used on school blackboards, and coat the inside of the collar where the rings are. The chalk does a very easy trick; absorbs the body oil from the ring. A hardy scrubbing with a solution of shampoo (which is also designed to cut body oils) and warm water should alleviate the rings.

Mud will usually not stain if washed soon enough. Knock off any dried, large sections of mud. Use a sponge and dish-washing liquid to attack what remains. You should then wash the garment normally, as soon as possible.

Quick hints about stains:

If it's a greasy stain (such as mayonnaise, animal fat, oil, etc.) always try a grease solvent first.

Egg whites will loosen sticky substances such as chewing gum.

For really bad rust stains, try a little old fashioned cream of tartar.

Diluted rubbing alcohol will usually lift hard-to-clean stains such as shoe polish, but it may loosen the garment color as well.

A mild peroxide solution will usually lift scorch marks from an iron.

Always try out stain removers on an unseen part of the garment, such as the inside hem, or on seam material. Many solvents and cleaners are too strong for certain fabrics, especially delicate ones and synthetics.

The color-fastness and the washability of a fabric, plus the fiber content, determine how you should go about "attacking" a stain.

If, while trying to remove a spot, bleeding occurs, it can usually be halted by adding white vinegar to the water and rinsing the garment.

Lemon juice is a great stain remover, but it is also a natural bleach! Be careful when using it.

Most floor wax stains will wash out. Simply add extra detergent to the stain and double rinse.

Catsup is not impossible to remove if attacked quickly. A little glycerine will soften it, and should be followed by a mild soap and water scrub.

When using "hard" cleaners such as ammonia, try applying them with an eye-dropper to restrict the amount used.

Always work near a source of running water when removing stains to allow you to flush the garment in case the solvent you're working with reacts badly to the fabric.

Old toothbrushes, cheese-cloths, and butter knives all make invaluable tools when removing stains.

No matter what cleaning agent you use, always remember to rinse it out completely before ironing the garment.

THE LAUNDRY

Although most of us would not hesitate to spend any amount on skin care, we are hesitant to do the same for our clothing. Just like skin, though, our clothes do not really need a host of fancy cleaning aids with catchy names and high price-tags; they need the attention of soap and water and a little personal care. Clothes that are well cared for are clothes that last a long time. Well cared-for clothing retains its shape and smartness for years. After all, to be considered well-dressed, is to be considered well-groomed. Our clothing, when it is clean and obviously cared for with respect helps to present a good impression. Also, the rising price of clothing today makes us consider each piece an investment. An ill-cared for piece of property returns nothing on its investment.

Just as dirt and germs attack our skin and cause the cells to be worn away, so do they attack clothing. Dirty clothing wears out quicker, just as dirty skin creases and erupts in blemishes. In this chapter, we've compiled hints on how to do laundry, some hints on clothing maintenance, and some smart tips on how to attack specific kinds of dirt.

You can wash delicate things without worry in your machine. When you're ready to wash delicate articles, simply place them inside an old cotton pillowcase, and use a piece of string to tie it closed! The pillowcase will absorb the "shock" from machine laundering and clean your delicates without hand washing. You should still set your machine on "gentle", though.

Vinegar should be in the final rinse. White vinegar, about a cup, in the final rinse of your wash, rids them of any excess suds or soap deposits. It will also soften your clothes naturally, without expensive fabric softeners.

Shampoo makes a great laundry detergent, especially on areas of accumulated body grime. Shampoos, you see, are formulated to cut through natural body oils. You may find them especially effective for hand laundering.

Add a little ammonia to your whites. They'll sparkle and smell fresh if you add about a quarter cup to your wash cycle. Be careful when adding it to delicate or brightly colored clothes, as they may fade.

Instead of bleaching, try this: the next time you have stained or heavily soiled whites, add half a cup of lemon juice to the water you use to wash them. You'll have to use very hot water, so rule out all delicates.

Try this in the rinse. Pour in a little cream rinse (for hair) the next time you do washable woolens. Add it during the final rinse. You'll be pleasantly surprised at how soft and fragrant your clothes come out.

Even your washer needs to be washed once in a while. Soap film and scum build up easily in washers. If you're like us, though, you haven't got the time or desire to scrub the inside of your washer. Instead, run the machine on hot water, normal cycle, and add a bottle of vinegar. It'll clean your machine in no time flat.

Always following washing instructions. The U.S. Government requires all manufacturers to print fabric content and washing instructions. Pay attention to them. The manufacturers may recommend certain treatments for cleaning garments, and they don't do it for their health. They do considerable research on the best care for their fabrics, and we should take advantage of them. Proper care will add years to the life of any garment.

Borax works wonders on bed linens, handkerchiefs, and undergarments. Not only will it whiten and brighten them, but it will also add a fresh, clean smell. Borax "hardens" the surface of fabrics, too, so that they withstand soil and grime better.

Chamois and doeskin are washable. They react well to hand washing in a mild, sudsy solution of warm water and soap. A few drops of olive oil in the rinse water will soften them again.

Most woolen blankets should be dry-

cleaned. You can, however, wash them yourself at home if you keep a few things in mind.

Don't add detergent (which should be very mild) until the blanket is thoroughly saturated with water.

Add only a little detergent.

Wash the blanket only a minute or a minute and a half. Rinse it for no more than four minutes.

Dry it in a cool dryer or spin. A hot dryer will shrink it. Don't dry it completely.

If you line-dry your clothing, remember this: always dry bright colors inside out. This keeps them from fading. If possible, your clothes-line should be placed in the shade, at least partially.

When hand-washing lace, try this: wrap the lace around a clean, empty soda bottle. It'll be easy to see if you're getting the lace clean, and it'll be far harder to snag it.

Here's a tip for starch users. If you starch your clothes, you should know that starch builds up on the rim of the iron you use to press them. You can't exactly wash an iron, but there is an easy to remove the build-up. Heat your iron to a high heat, or set it on "cotton". Now, simply "iron" an old paper bag by running your hot iron over it. The excess starch will be deposited on the brown bag.

Your ironing board cover gets dirty, too. Like everything else, it needs to be laundered occasionally. You can keep it cleaner longer, though, very easily. When not in use, cover the top with old dry-cleaner's plastic bags. They'll easily stretch over the surface and protect the cover from dust.

You might also spray your cover with spray starch. Starch helps fabric resist dirt longer.

Pleated skirts are a cinch to iron with this tip. Simply pin the pleats in place onto the top of the ironing board. Press them from top to bottom, never pressing more than four or five pleats at a time. Remember where your pins are, though, and don't press over them!

You can hand-wash knit scarves, gloves, hats, and mittens. Hand-washing won't hurt them, and you'll find it more economical than dry-cleaning. Be sure that when you dry them, you don't hang them. Knit accessories should be blocked; layed out flat and returned to the proper shape by flattening and shaping with your fingers.

Clothes smell fresher when dried on a clothes-line. Clothes line drying always brings back a note of nostalgia, of a slower-paced America. There is no reason why you can't still use a line and dry clothes in the open air. If you do, however, you should be aware of certain things:

An old-fashioned rope clothesline may evoke memories, but the elements will rot it.

A wire clothes-line will serve your needs, but to keep from rusting, you should shellack it once a year.

They come in plastic now, old-fashioned wooden clothespins will do the job. Before you put them out in the weather, though, here's a quick tip for acclimating them. Boil them in vinegar and water, and then let stand until the water cools. This process strengthens and hardens the wood.

Here's a quick guide for separating your laundry:

Separate all white and pale, color-fast clothing into one pile.

Make a second pile of all dark clothing that's color-fast.

All darks that will run can be done together as long as they are all similar in color.

Make a pile of delicate things and hand washables.

Wash all new things that you are un-sure of separately.

Make a pile of clothes that are stained and need special care.

New towels are wonderful, but don't forget they're new when you wash them. New cotton towels, especially dark or bright colors always "bleed", so it is best to wash them alone at least for the first few times.

When a tag says "Dry Clean Only", there's a reason for it. Although the fabric looks like fabric you've washed before, the eye isn't always the best judge. Cottons that say dry-clean only may be heavily "sized"; fabric sizing would be lost during washing and you'd be left with a limp rag instead of the garment you loved. Also, the cloth used may not have been pre-shrunk which means that if it's washed, it may shrink until it's unwearable. If you love your clothing, obey the care tags.

It's always best to underdry. Over drying of clothing, sheets, or blankets causes unnecessary puckering and is hard on the shape and fabric in general. Under dry your shirts and immediately put them on a hanger to finish air-drying. You'll find they wrinkle less and retain their shape better, which means they'll need less ironing. Many will only require a quick "finger-pressing".

Always remember this when hand-washing delicates: remove your rings and jewelry. Many of our friends have snagged precious articles of clothing, ruining them, because they forgot to take off their rings. Rubber gloves are probably the best suggestion of all.

Here's a tip when drying blankets, or other large heavy items. Always throw a few towels into the dryer, too. They'll cut down on drying time and cushion the blankets).

Silk can be hand-washed. You should be careful not to use too harsh a detergent. We believe that a really mild soap, such as castille, is best. It is also good to avoid scrubbing the silk as much as possible. Use your hands to act as an agitator; stains should be handled separately. Never let silk soak very long, in either soapy water or clear, and be careful not to wring it dry. Use a towel to blot up excess moisture.

You may also press silk. We've found that silk presses best with a cool iron. You should never touch the silk with the hot iron directly. Lay a dampened, linen-cloth over the silk and iron through it.

Quick hints for the laundry:

Never hang a sweater to dry; block it on a flat surface to maintain its shape and fit.

Corduroy can be hand-washed. Electric dryers actually restore the flattened nap and are good for the cloth.

To speed the drying of hand-washables, gently roll them in a towel and blot. It'll cut your drying time in two.

Make sure zippers are up before pants are washed to prevent snags.

Feather pillows can be hand-washed; the bath-tub is the ideal container.

Hot water and excessive soaking are really hard on non-color-fast clothing.

Salt is great additive to the rinse. It sets the colors of dark clothing.

Never hang knit-wear from a clothes-line.

Shrunken woolens may "loosen" and stretch if soaked in a creme rinse used for hair care.

TAKING CARE OF YOUR HOME

A house will probably be the major investment of your lifetime; it will most certainly be somewhere near the top of your list, we're sure. Like the old saying, "A house is not a home . . .", your house won't become your home without love, care, and a highly personal touch. Just as a child cannot grow without the proper care, your home will not grow, much less last, without respect and maintenance. We aren't saying that you need to devote your life to the upkeep of your home (although most of us do), or even that you are capable of doing all the major repairs. Our point is that we know that all of us are capable of doing a great many of the easier chores, and even some of the more difficult tasks, if we know how.

Consequently, we've included what we call both major and minor hints in this chapter. No, we are not suggesting you undertake the re-roofing job that's going to take a major bite out of your household budget. That is, unless you're in **very** good shape! There is no reason why you can't perform simple "fix-its", replacements, and have a working knowledge of the tools you'll need to accomplish them.

Organization may be the most important thing. A home runs more smoothly when it's in order. Start with your closets and drawers. Get rid of garments you don't wear or want. Put the medicine chest and linen closets in order; make sure household tools are all in one place and are easily accessible. Your cleaning tools, from vacuums to scrubbrushes should be organized and accessible. Designate one area to keep them all in and you'll never have to waste time frantically searching for some item you need. An organized home is less work for you to maintain in the long run.

Keep your tools from rusting. A good assortment of household tools is a must, but if you store them in the garage or basement, they can easily become damp and rusty. Tools are a large investment that are easy to maintain. If we don't maintain them properly, the investment is wasted. We discovered that if we placed several strips of ordinary chalk in the tool box, or other containers, it would absorb the moisture and keep everything rust free.

A little soap can go a long way. Before you try to hammer in a nail or put a new screw into something, try this little trick that a carpenter friend shared with us. Simply push the nail or screw through an old bar of soap. The nail or screw will drive easier and it won't split the wood.

Got a screw that won't loosen? Here's an easy trick that always works! Just heat the tip of your screwdriver and try again. It'll come loose easily this time.

If you're not used to working with plaster, you may find that it dries too fast. If so, simply add a little household vinegar to it, and you'll be able to work it longer until you get the hang of it.

You may split a plastic wall when you drive a nail in, but there is a way of sinking a nail without splitting your wall, too. Heat the nail with a match, first. The hot nail will go through the plaster easier and it won't put cracks in your lovely walls.

You may not have to sand your old, dark wood floors. There are several brands of high-powered floor soaps on the market today, that require only a little elbow grease, as opposed to the time, mess, and experience of sanding. You'll also find that scrubbing with this floor cleaner lightens your hard-wood and brightens it considerably.

Are your porcelain sinks chipped? Your hardware has special kits that are easy to use and return the porcelain or enamel to a condition that is almost new. These kits, incidentally, come in a variety of colors.

Leaky faucets cost you money. Although that small drip may seem inconsequential to you, you'll find it mirrored in your utility bill. Washers that will tighten your faucets and get rid of those leaks take only minutes to install.

You can replace defective light

switches yourself. The main thing to remember about working with electricity is to be careful. Concentrate fully on what you're doing. Begin by shutting down the main power switch. Loosen the screws that hold the switch cover and take off the plate. The switch will be loosened and you can gently pull it loose from its setting. Loosen the bolts holding the switch and remove it. Put on the new switch and return it to the wall. Tighten it and replace the switch cover.

Loose windows mean more than just an annoying rattle! They mean that your electric bills are escalating, too. Save your nerves and lower your fuel bills! Putty is simple to install and it'll be worth the investment in time later.

Do you have cracked windows? If your windows are cracked but not broken, here's a quick repair tip. Until you can afford to replace them, simply paint them with a thin coating of clear shellac.

Want to know how to clean your screens quickly? A vacuum, without any attachments will suck the dirt and dust off in seconds! You won't have to scrub them, or even take them off your windows.

Do you have small holes in your screens? Don't replace the whole screen. "Paint" the small ones with model airplane glue and they'll be invisible and sealed.

If you save newspapers, beware of insects. Stack them neatly, but throw a few mothballs inside them. You won't have to worry then about providing a home for pests.

Ever wondered how to find a wall stud when you want to hang a picture? Wall studs are usually sixteen and eighteen inches apart. Tap the wall gently with a hammer. The change in sound will indicate the presence of a stud.

Tired of squeaky hinges? Instead of messy oiling, or replacing the hinges or screws, try spraying on a little of the non-stick cooking sprays. They're inexpensive, and they work like a charm.

Do your tables or chairs wobble? Well, whatever you do, don't try shortening the three other legs to try matching the length of the one that wobbles. Soon, you'll feel as if you're trapped in an old "Laurel and Hardy" film! Instead, try **adding** a little plastic wood to the short leg and building it up. You can always sand it down if it is too tall.

Before you drive in a nail to hang a picture, read this! Don't mar your walls with several useless holes from nails, because you didn't like the way a picture looked once it was up. Instead, have someone hold the picture in various spots until you get a feel of where it looks best in the room.

If you have no one to help you, here's a helpful hint. Simply cut a shape out of colored construction paper. Use a straight pin to hold it on the wall. A straight pin's hole won't mar the surface.

You can finish unfinished picture frames yourself. You can stain them with shoe polish in a variety of shades.

Old ice-cube trays make great organizers. You can store washers, screws, carpet tacks, small nails, and nuts and bolts in them. That way, you'll always know where they are.

Keep your tools clean. Dirty tools soon lose their edge and often rust. A quick wiping with an oiled rag is usually sufficient to clean them. Never clean them with soap and water.

Quick tips for household repairs:

Never nail down loose linoleum. Use glue to replace loosened tiles.

Fluorescent lights that darken may only need the ends reversed to extend their life.

Before driving a nail into plaster, make an "X" of scotch tape and your nail has a better chance of not splitting the plaster.

Pour a little club soda on a rusted bolt to loosen it. Ammonia will also work.